"For Those Who Love, There Is Poetry..."

"For Those Who Love, There Is Poetry . . ."

Charles HunnaHustla

Library of Congress Control Number: 2016902964
ISBN: Hardcover   978-1-5144-6939-2
                Softcover   978-1-5144-6938-5

Print information available on the last page.

Rev. date: 02/24/2016

To order additional copies of this book, contact:
Xlibris
1-888-795-4274
www.Xlibris.com
Orders@Xlibris.com
733372

This work is dedicated to the writers, poets, artists, and the many other creative minds on Instagram whose own endeavors are an inspiration.

CONTENTS

Introduction

Woman Arise!

Yes!
You are Goddess!
Mother Nature's sweet Caress
Her every step, every word, her truth you are
God's gift, His best, nothing less, tenderness
Seize your time, arrest man's mad made quest
His blind rush, path headin', toward Armageddon
Spread your beauty, your peace, your togetherness
Confess!
Here to heal, to bless
To thwart his wars and recklessness
His fuss, lack of trust, silence his blunderbuss
Blunt his thrust
Woman
Hear his thunder, waken from your slumber
Don your God-given cape, let love escape
Men's weapons rust
And
Save us . . .

—HunnaHustla

Would Ever Let Go

"If I relent
Let you hold my hand
Would you ever let go?"
Her words like a mist crept in places only I had known
Enclosing her hand as dark does night in my own
I of course said, "No . . ."
Her laughter rung and after all this time
Her hand still seems held in mine
At my lips yearning to kiss her fingers
At her vanity where her scent yet lingers
I long to touch her reflection mirrored
Though still to this day
I cannot sleep in the bed where she once lay
So what is this hell I live you may wonder of
Read all my cruel heartless memories answer love . . .

—HunnaHustla

. . . And When We Meet . . .

We will know us when we meet
Having seen us countless times
Out of lonely thoughtful reach
Having heard our footsteps light as snow
Falling in dreams we have yet to sow
We will know us by the laughter in our eyes when we meet
By the words we bring in the wisdom of hearts we keep
By the feel of our touch in the silence we speak
We will know by the lilt of our voices in the way we greet
Having formed in our minds the ways of our kind
We will know by a kiss so sweet
Yes we will know us when we meet
And when we meet
We will know . . .

—HunnaHustla

Of How You've Touched . . .

As this, my restless mind, weeps
I tread while city sleeps
My life steps unheard along its streets
Attracting glares of blackened white wheels
Wandering debris-strewn fields of long dead flesh
Time stops to examine light of its breath
Night awakens to wrath of invisible days
An unseen hand lifts veil of its ways
Moans deep into my steepening pain

"Your tears cascading beneath my stars shall leave no stain"

Staring awestruck with unrelenting gaze
I recall we met where moonlight stays
Your eyes spoke the fears of falling dew
Yearning to say without saying what we both knew
I dared embrace you
Now
My heart rages against my chest for loss of your heart's beat
My lips swearing never to taste lips as yours so sweet
Rebel against me
My soul irks my spirit because it hurt yours
Loving you is needing you and loving you much
Here I write with my blood how you have touched . . .

—HunnaHustla

Perhaps Always . . .

Thought of you today / though wish I hadn't
Uncovered your picture
Your eyes
Your smile
Your memory
The laughter we shared
Longed for you today / though wish I hadn't
Opened this wound
This burden
This caring
This wanting you
Still
Thought of you today
Perhaps always will . . .

—HunnaHustla

The Model and the Eyesore

An eyesore
Shuttered, condemned, by smoldering, angry fires
Peering through jagged holes in its roof, chopped by ax of hateful
desires
Sighs at sight of its graffiti-scarred walls, spattered stains,
jackhammered urinals
Straining drains, shattered pieces like Roman ruins, littering its floor
with dread
Pains a spray-painted blackbird perched beneath a windowless ledge
Back swayed against a lifeless tree, symbolic of a people once free
Undaunted, stepping like a goddess into charred remains
Shedding her silken blouse upon mounds of soot off streets
The model straightens her black winged crown of gold
Elegant hands telling a story oft told, her life unfolds
She looks away as the cameras roll
Whispering "Art! Art I see!"
The eyesore weeps . . .

—HunnaHustla

We Were Laughter

Together we defined laughter
Laughter without pause, long, loud guffaws
Never heeding the stares, looks of alarm
The open, disapproving jaws
At even them we laughed
Tacking them on like sticky-note laws
To the cause of our laughter in the first place
Hers, beginning in her eyes
Escaped to their corners and tickled her face
Until her eyes were almost shut
Kept open only by her flowing tears
Our voices grew hoarse with laughter
Our bodies bent over with it, stomachs ached
So very long ago, whenever I think of her, though
The first thing I do is laugh . . .

—HunnaHustla

Change . . .

Change
An avenging sword, comes
Not to slay pains of past within you
But to shred their shadows in which you linger
Lest even from you they veil gain in secrets you harbor
Change comes to reveal your strength in imagined weakness
As that weakness mere figment diluting your achievement
Convincing your heart its goals lay drained
Change
An avenging sword, comes
Not as hope, for hope sustains
But as dreams you dare not abandon
To that self your wounded past ingrained
Thus embrace this change as one ordained
Allow your long-held dreams remain
Unchained . . .

—HunnaHustla

Guest Poet: Jean Bascom

"Writing is archeology—digging the bones of belief from the soul's bedrock."

—Jean Bascom

Changing Clothes

Cinderella had only to wash her dirty little
Hands and put on a new dress to find that
Appearances enhance and solidify our shifting
Notions of self. Fashion makes us all Fairy
Godmothers. With the seamstress's spell we
Invent ourselves over and again by lowering
Necklines, raising hems, tightening laces.
Glass slippers give way to buckled biker boots.

Choose your clothes carefully and transform!
Linen, cotton, lace, silk, leather—magic words,
Old magic, whispered in fabric voices by the
Touch of cloth to cloth and cloth to skin . . .
Have you slipped on a flowing white dress and
Escaped to a flowered meadow? Or let a short
Skirt turn you fierce? Go on—midnight's coming.

—Jean Bascom

No Promises

Nothing stirred—not a twig or a leaf—in the
Oak tree. It stood silent, without expectations

Presently, the wind came: it whooshed, it
Rushed, it thrilled through the branches of the
Oak with a delightful unplanned rustling,
Making merry. And then it blew on, with no
Intent in its departure—as free to go as it was to
Stay. The oak shivered in its wake, then settled
Easily back into silent being—not hoping, not
Seeking the next breeze, not anything but a tree.

—Jean Bascom

Retreat

I

Recoiling like a serpent after the strike, I
Eye my emotions from a distance, safely
Tucking myself into the loops of intellect.
Reasonable—that's what I'll be, full of
Easy logic, feeling little. A bright-eyed
Adder, venom in the hissing bite; but coiled
Tight in the mind's dark basket, almost safe.

II

Routed on the battlefield, my emotions scatter. A few remain
Entrenched—those best trained, but not necessarily strongest.
Tanks roll in, the heavy artillery: intellect, driving through the
Ranks, mowing down everything in its path. Heartache, passion,
Ecstasy flee at the approach of this armored force. Surrender!
Attack is futile. The soldiers are spent, ready to collapse and smoke
Their last packs of cigarettes in tents or hospitals or POW camps.

III

Rest in me, He says. As if sleep could heal
Everything. And maybe some sleeps can.
Truth comes in while we sleep, through dreams
Realer than reality, when the sleep is deep
Enough (and in His arms, it is). I'd like to fall
Asleep, listening to Him breathe, listening
To His heartbeat. Wondering what it means.

—Jean Bascom

Solitude

I

Secret places still hide, tucked away in this
Old earth: little glades of soft green moss,
Lichen-covered trees, and piles of stones
Imbued with an intimate magic. We
Take walks in the forest, unknowingly trying to
Unearth these sacred spots—silent places to
Discover the secrets of our hearts that nature
Evokes in ways no cathedral or library can.

II

Speak to me in whispers, as if speaking
Only to yourself. Speak so softly that
Lies are lost beneath your breath, and dim,
Intimate truths—the ones you seem to
Taste rather than tell—pass like a kiss
Under your teeth, through your lips,
Directly into my mouth. Place your secrets—
Even the dark ones—on my tongue, as my own.

III

So still, this tree-lined lake, reflecting the blue
Opinion of a spring sky, cloudless and certain.
Light pauses here, and breeze—the elements
Inhaling, breath held in anticipation of some
Truth about to . . . there! Look: rippling
Under the surface, stirring the scene, a fish
Dances alone and leaps—startling the water,
Emerging like realization on a thoughtful face.

—Jean Bascom

Wind Chimes

I

Woo me, pull me in, laughing. Take my hand,
Insisting I twirl and sway. Carry me away to soft
Naked places. I am the chimes, you the wind.
Dance me to your silent music, make me sing.
Change my stillness to movement, free and
Happy. I am waiting, heavily hanging, my potential
Inviting your touch. Touch me. Touch me. Set me in
Motion. You are the breeze, caressing, kissing
Every mouth you meet—mouths of wildflowers,
Ships sails, kites, branching trees. Why not kiss me?

II

Wordless songs ring from the wind's throat,
Inviting birds and insects to take up the
Notes. The long, glinting columns quiver, sway.
Dance a silver shimmy against one another.
Charms are recited in this old, unwritten,
Hidden language—this voice that compels
Imagination, carrying those who understand to
Memory's distant island, or to some unseen
Elsewhere compiled from worlds of fairy tales.
Somewhere only heard of, where no one's been.

III

Whirling in the breeze, they tremble and sing,
In the way of all soft wild things that wind
Notices: flowers, insect wings, fur, leaves.
Dancers full of uninhibited laughter, briefly
Charged with echoes of voices far away or gone,
Hear them tap their glinting feet. He listens,
Imagining her with him, and closes his eyes,
Mesmerized by the suggestive voice of chimes.
Each reverberation prompts a smile, but too
Soon the wind stills, the bells and her face fade.

—Jean Bascom

HunnaHustla

Forever Ending . . .

I alone inhabiting this world of two suns
One setting behind hills of mistakes at the base of my trash can
The other rising from the dark in my pen
Saw, as if an enemy, thoughts of her arraying themselves against me
An army of regret wading across motes of lies,
storming castles of truth to ask why
We, like strangers, walked side by side, each
desiring to not again be left behind
We searched for hope, a savior of some
kind, yet still our love drowned
She perhaps not wanting to be alone with her thoughts
Snatched at each spoken one of mine
Our laughter rung bells of silence, words
hung hollow as veils across night
Having vowed love countless chances, we
both fell to other lover's glances
She wept as tears died behind my eyes, our souls rending
Not wanting to recognize
Forever loves are forever ending . . .

—HunnaHustla

Their Pain . . . Be My Pain . . .

Like an uninvited stealthy guest
While in dark of early morning they rest
I wander among words that attest
To their struggles with loneliness
Revealing open wounds, some borne upon silver spoons
Jaded tongues spewing as gaseous sewers in cities old
Tell of hearts once bowed to lovers of extraordinary hold
Clay-footed messiahs in platinum and gold
Who also treaded lightly lest they weep
Love-stained ink writing of losing whom they seek
Searching wide and deep for the one of which they reek,
Yielding such madness and broken parts
I vow to rend my poet soul
To touch and mend their shrunken hearts
For among their many ruins have I found this one be true
That in the shedding of their love
Even their tortured love
None but evil gain
And that evil knows their pain
Be my pain
Too . . .

—HunnaHustla

A Poem for My Muse

Picture her with a whip in her hand
Not leather, sand, not cracked, lipped
A literary offering sipped
Like stars bucked and dripped
Her words, my rhyme, she whispers fine lines
Sweet as a female spine, toxic to unschooled minds
Making me write her speech in Greek
She wreaks the rhythm of cosmic geeks
My muse don't twerk but she a freak
Sapiosexual beyond complete
Just last night she beat my WHAT?
Don't get it twisted, she realistic, mental gym (nistic)
WORD! She hissed it, waxing poetic, being unapologetic
Love my muse, love the music she use
Sometimes jazz, sometimes blues
Not blastin', lastin', till vegans stop fastin'
Fusing me, musing me
Nonstop doo-wop

—HunnaHustla

All of These . . .

I love the lonely, the alone
Solitary rain-wet trees
Random thoughts, sun-setting Sundays
Crashing waves and windblown leaves
Sweetened lips, summer breeze, all of these
I love in you . . .

—HunnaHustla

Her Favorite Mistake

She was all that
Hand holding and laughter
Summertime and thereafter
Dimples and white teeth
Cali in June, bright smiles, and perfume
She was coke when coke was coke, when ganja a two hit toke
Even though my mind heated, she took it away, said I didn't need it
She was give and take, chocolate cake, not
a single calorie fake, bootie shake
Not twerk, quake, all that and my favorite
mistake, she tolerated mine for love's sake
I cheated, she pleaded, then walked, I talked,
said I didn't mean it, was just a stalk
"Too little, too late, your bad, don't hate," she said
"You can be my favorite mistake . . ."

—HunnaHustla

Diana ... Eternal Princess

I sit upon a fence of red brick and concrete
Fronting the yard of home
A fading, falling, purpling sun sets warm against my back
Swirling winds toss soothing sprays of watering lawns
Rustles uncut grasses green and gold
A leaf, long fallen, tumbling over
Whispers low her name
Diana . . .
Echoes deep within my soul
Hushing sounds of nature's yearnings
Awakening love, feelings old
Now
New memories forgotten
Chance amour's fleeting lures unveil as ale-passion-mates
Bursts of ardent mysteries lost mid our haste were they
Crystal chameleons, she may have painted as charmers
Perhaps titled "In the Artful Way of Us" by Di
I wish had been an us in we, I would have spoken
Of an endless longing, burning unknown
Like fireplace fantasies lit in rustic cabins
We brewed snowcapped mountain rendezvous
Met slumber-less early dawns
Late afternoon Sundays
Her palace or mine

Among barren trees whose shadows roam
Within my thoughts of her
I watched twilight vie with moody sky to be her crown
I saw dust clouds shy from her
A flowered garden, the scent of her
In regal silence bowed
I felt the air moan as she set sail upon an ocean
Wept of its salt for her

And I brooded that all her time enthroned
She fed hours of love-filled minutes to every second
While I sat rapt at foot of God
Writing knighthood fable, medieval sonnet
Vowing ever to poet life for her
To even in death lyric on for her
Still my heart sighs broken as dark descends
On her day of surrender
And though of her needless ruin my spirit proclaims
That far beyond where Camelot reigns
A greater world cries serene her gifts remain
I in remembrance of her one brief moment
I sing a love song for peace, recite a death chant for hate
I pray the wounded earth curse not in stone her pain . . .

—HunnaHustla

Guest Poet: Fabienne Casseus

"Hurricane, in the form of woman, with the rest, I am words."

—Fabienne Casseus

Battlefield

you were making war with yourself,
and I walked into center field.
I learned these witch songs from you.
but you said you'd never burn.
what happens now?
for Pete's sake, we're both choking!

"dance with me,"
you say,
"on Orion's belt,
and laugh with Galileo
until we forget
about these elephants
in our chests."

—Fabienne Casseus

Fire Escape

my love,
you'll find me
muddled underneath mud.
adorning my ash-filled lungs
with seaweeds
and handpicked thorns.
i'm flushed inside these ocean storms.
and sleeping in moon dust baths—
i waddle in knee-deep in the oils of my virgin thoughts.
draw me in with the fragrance of your mouth,
and chase down my shadows.
let's be drunk.
and lovely.
and merry.
on the wine of our truths.
marry me in the lake of our naive youth.
make me keeper of your rafters,
and you take guard
of my nights like firewood.
baby,
spare me the brute of your spine.
cut my tongue and leave me paper white.
make timid lies of all my exit plans;
your eyes were my only fire escape.

—Fabienne Casseus

Ordidnary

In the kitchen my knife
splits a grapefruit into thirds
and I am perched on my toes in false stiletto.
under my sole the earth shifts.
tonight I am a slug with stilt patterns on my skin
with a burnished gold mouth.
but I was once velvet.
I promise when I whispered to myself that night,
while the moon was playing coy
perching herself like a comma on your lips,
I didn't mean to play the wise oak.
but I said kiss me.
I meant, pull down Apollo
and cover me with song.
but I said listen.
I meant, close your eyes
because I do not say the words that rest
on my heart in the dark
and lastly,
I was silent.
I meant to tell you
(but I didn't)
about the times I slept with the windows open
only to see if I could pick out your voice from the cricket's song.
I loved you in my first tongue,
instinctual, native, and with a fever.
how are you counting your future now?
standing by the water watching the lord walk?
filling your slop buckets with the greyhound's tongue?
you should have dug deeper.
I am in a cluster of indigo pearls inside
an oyster of playing the dotish wife.
you wouldn't recognize me.

I'm all hands cascading into too much height
with outstretched ostrich wings with spring heat.
I keep plums in my hair.
and dirt under my nails.
I find beauty in the ordinary.
and lover,
we are nothing special.
ashes inside glass skin with silver buttons
chanting little rhymes on our steamboat.
did it matter?
you still played yo-yo with the afterlife
and I got high on your polished floors.
our panther skin would still break apart under moonlight.

—Fabienne Casseus

Warrior's Song

please be soft,
the warrior in me is on her bad left feet.
the whole day filled her with devils.
her breasts hang like a woman,
but her laugh is still a child.
she comes to warm her jagged angles,
against the lazy sensuality of moonlight.

—Fabienne Casseus

La Bête Noir

in your attic,
there is a woman,
sweeping the ceilings with her hair
and mopping the floors with her hands.
you will meet her only once.
she ties wicks around her ankles
and keeps a rope for a tongue.
she speaks in gritty sand language of finite spaces.
she peers at you then wets the sheets over your eyes.
my mother says I should only feed her at dusk.
my mother says she is swallowing grief slowly.
my mother says the weight of the hem of her skirt
keeps her head from floating.
she keeps seagulls in her throats.
she does only what your shadows whisper to her
after you turn your back .
she shivers when she smiles, and
then she lifts her skirt and breaks into a run
she is a stallion at the feet.
she's scraggly and blood matted,
rolling and tucking beneath the belly
moving in cadence to the howling silence.

—Fabienne Casseus

HunnaHustla

In the Wee Hours . . .

Sleep laughs and leaves me at three in the morning
The hour that I laughed as you left
The hour when dreams of you
Morph into nightmare
That is when your place in bed is coldest beside me
Then is when I caress where your body once rested
That is when scent of you
Haunts and chills
That is when I reflect upon the last chance you gave
Then is when I wonder, "A chance or a challenge?"
If a chance, I didn't take it
If a challenge, I didn't win
But that is what I wish you were here to answer . . .

—HunnaHustla

Love Storm

Thunder cracking harder than a forty-year-old virgin
On the night he's been waiting for
Lightning illuminating downpour, I stand at patio door
Watching summer rain memories of you, doubting we're through
As hints are like flirts, they never ring true
His words, do they stimulate your thoughts, as mine used to
Do they caress your mind, does his voice, like my own, soothe you
One man's traction being another man's skid
Has he ever dreamed your dreams as I once did
If you see him again, will he yet be your
lover, as well as your friend
Will he be by your side at time's end?
I touch a single raindrop upon my face, savor a salty taste
Fading into distant past, reminding love's tempestuous storms
Never last
Still, as if embracing you, I hold them fast . . .

—HunnaHustla

Neither Nor, Either Or

Not since you
Are these thoughts
Ever mine
Nor this heart
Neither mine
Or this soul
This being
This life
Since you
These ways
Are never mine . . .

—HunnaHustla

Of Heart, Gravity, Spirit

A stolen heart / suffers not its thief
A fallen rose / despises gravity
Yet a broken spirit / swallows sorrow

—HunnaHustla

Ode to My Instagram Followers

In wee hours of my world / I journey through yours
Seeking word from your soul / a phrase from your heart
Finds harbor in my mind / where your restless longings
Wordings of hopes and pain / fuels mine unrestrained
Unchained / earth one day shall reign in peace you say
Those who know it poet / of long-gone loves lingering on
Quills swearing never again / spirits vowing ever more
I dwell till dark's light breaks against reverie's shore
Awash among waves of unreceding feelings
I conceding / you do not follow me
Needing / I follow you . . .

—HunnaHustla

Your Words, Music

"Muse, everywhere, find another and use it . . ."
Your words, music, still your leaving I can't excuse it
As my heart, smitten, lives where poems are written
Where in beating for you, when you had come,
It had known there is no other as you are from
"And if another like me, then I am she . . ."
Your words, music, still your leaving I can't excuse it
For why pierce my soul
Your love
Only to leave me with memories of?

—HunnaHustla

Her Keepsake

He loved her crooked smile
The one she smiled whenever he joked
She half-closed her eyes whenever she spoke
Of their learning to smoke beneath an oak
Where their names are yoked
She had wondered whether its soul pained
A caring he felt she feigned
As she had carved their initials deep
Had taken the shavings to keep
Now of her love bereft
Clinging to what is left
He envisions her smile
And weeps . . .

—HunnaHustla

Guest Poet: Allison Theresa

"I could just write about pain, but I'd rather explain the ecstasy of it."

—Allison Theresa

Lucid

How painful it is to find yourself drowning in lucid dreams
of promises made in past lives
To walk against the water with petals of dried roses as
stepping-stones
How painful it is to hear the faint voices of soul mates
calling out to you
unable to distinguish one from the other.
To smell the clouds and taste the earth between your lips
How painful to relive heartbreak
How painful to relive a life forgotten
But how sweet in dreaming of promise

—Allison Theresa

Molasses

I am a slave to the sweet, numbing slumber of your
molasses-laden heart,
and despite the fight I put up, I am planted at your feet and
feeding from your roots.
I cave in at the taste of your lonely soul and dream of
nourishing your emptiness.
I dream and dream of you, with eyes wide open to even
the most evil within you.
I feed and feed from you, all that you are and all that you
hide from me.
Despite the fight I put up, I fill my ladle and drink and drink
of you.

—Allison Theresa

Promise

I loved you despite the stars you promised me would fall
gently into my palms,
but they simply disappeared.
I loved you despite the ocean breeze you promised to
capture in a bottle,
but the tide carried it away.
I loved you despite your promise of an everlasting sunrise,
but your leaving cast a shadow over the light forever.
Now all I feel are voids where stars should be.
Now all I hear are waves with no hellos.
Now all I see is a dark sun, circling around all these
broken promises.

—Allison Theresa

Rabbit Hole

You meet me in the middle of every night
where my stark, grim realities and nasty,
chokehold fantasies live. You are welcomed to
wander there, though you only meet me
halfway. Your safe space fears the passion
behind my eyes and the lust beneath my
tongue. You draw closer each time but pull
back, never wanting to fully submerge in my
black and white words that lead to the
unknown colorful toxicity of me.

—Allison Theresa

The Pained Life

We stopped time with our tears and
exploded stars with our screams, but
no one noticed, and no one saw how
we shattered alone in a room.
We were well beyond saving because
we clung to the pain like it was
keeping us alive.

—Allison Theresa

HunnaHustla

Where Yet We Knew Us When

While soothing my mind's eye I viewed
Caravanning scenes of you
I was imbued with a memory
Of our having met before we met
Though as with a trend seems I forget
Where yet we knew us when

Perhaps running free before time was set
I had said of our meeting, yet
I saw along an endless spirit road
Where our naked souls
Yearning earth abode
Dreamt lives to live, songs to give
Although dreading their day of departing

For there had God conceived of us
In thunderous moans of lonely lust
As I remember His windswept tears of rain
Played blues in lightning's veins
Lit blushing hues in bows so fair
It pained the night to gain its dark
Thus dark forsook led sleep to light
In our hopes with heartfelt aims
From there it's clear where we deign
Where yet we knew us when

Where silent as a reverie
Within His breath, He had given me
A sense of knowing ahead your call to share this memory
Of our having met before we met
Lest now and then should we forget
Where yet we knew us when . . .

—HunnaHustla

Unseen Love . . .

I wonder
Might gravitational pull of earth keep us apart
Or is distance now incarnate standing between
I wonder could time be the evil of our divide
And since we being of water know ebb and tide
Perhaps moon's effect upon ocean be the fiend
Or maybe night is a blinding light
Day, a darkening sight to love
Causing eyes to not see
So the other to not be
Thus we beseech god's will and might
For what are we
Without a love
That feels right?

—HunnaHustla

Where Hesitation Looms, It Dooms . . .

Across the room
An untouched glass of wine he dines
He pretending not to feel her in his mind
Though intensity of her gaze intensifying
Burning his core, changing him
Better than ever was
Or as he concedes
Will ever be
Still he thinks her not his kind
While she
More alone than he
Wonders if ever to know again
That feeling gone . . .

—HunnaHustla

This Heart Freed

A Goddess, she
Once stood over me
Her words falling as gold dust
Petals of rose musk
Picture I beneath her scented poses
Yearning she release my heart before it closes
Yet its incarceration deemed just
My imagination's imprisoned lust
Cried out for one last touch
Now though free of her heart's murmur
May I once again
Not asking much
Long for her?

—HunnaHustla

My Whirlwind Muse

As if a blustery San Diego breeze, she blew into my life
Floored me like 'Frisco grog, spewed onto
streets wrapped in Beijing smog
Her voluptuous hips pushed into my mind,
climbed aboard my thoughts
Inspired a new phrase about her sway, demanded
I write without thinking or say
The tone of her poetry being also that way,
drew me like a magnet to her words
They smiled, winked, taunted across the page,
enticing me to join their parade
Together we beat drums, trumpeted, collaborated rhythm and spiel
Sapiosexual butt-naked zeal,
I clutched my groin, and she laughed, said she's not even real
Yet a part of my better half still, here solely
to influence a literary meal
"Although true I am woman," she cooed,
"You should know I am only your muse
Now awaken to the ocean lapping your heel
Poet
Describe to the world what you are given to feel . . ."

—HunnaHustla

50

The Harbinger

She laid black roses in his box
Blacker than black volcanic rocks
Blacker than the black of her dreadlocks
Blacker than the mourning of mourner's there
Her eyes blackened my mind beyond repair
The chopper she rode, the way she stared
Blacker than the leather she chose to wear
Sounding as blackbirds cawing the air
Blew black smoke until no one spared
Coughing up soot as lungs were snared
Those who scattered were those who cared
Who was black and who was fair
The dead man rose, she stroked his chin
He sang, "Color doesn't matter where I have been . . ."
Riding off on her chopper she shouted
"Now it begins!"

—HunnaHustla

Guest Poet: Maureen Alexandra

"Free-spirited woman looking to write away my conservative anchor and touch souls."

—Maureen Alexandra

Cinnamon Memories

There was a day filled with cinnamon,
spicy treats and spicy trysts.
The sea crashed outside our window
as we explored new territory.
panting, sweating.
What a beautiful mix,
salt air and body fluids.
Monet hung there looking at us,
trying to escape, no doubt.
Prison is hell.
Love is freedom.
Awkward glances
and hotel sheets are drugs.
Let's get higher and higher
in this heaven,
in cheap-art-cell hell.
Fucking damn!
This pleasure!
"You make me feel too good,
too good,
too good."
And even today, I die inside
knowing what was,
what could have been,
what cinnamon and sea air,
and fake Monets
can do to a soul.
It's just too beautiful to survive.
And I drown in memories
of waves crashing hard as we barely cum.

—Maureen Alexandra

Corpse

Thunder roared,
lightning lit up the crystal dimensions of that damn gaudy
chandelier from France.
"Expensive," he told me,
but I didn't care.
It was too big,
dripping with rhinestony droplets,
bleeding light onto the table
like a Halloween corpse cut from the neck.
My anger matched the distress of the thunder.
Each bolt, echoing my own angst,
each crack, whispering loudly in my soul.
"You fuckup," it shouts.
And as the reflection of the lightning on the crystal
chandelier
painted brilliant fireworks on my pale skin,
I silently prayed the lightning hit him too,
fix his fucked-up soul,
make him live once again.
I turned back to my book, *Frankenstein*,
and I occasionally gave
the light fixture above me
a gentle swing.

—Maureen Alexandra

Incense

I've had it!
Damn Marlboro blasts
haunt my dreams,
wrap their smoky arms
around my neck as I sleep,
choke all my senses dead,
fucking their memories
deep into my subconscious.
Damn Marlboros!
I hate them.
Too many suffocating dreams
tear through my thoughts.
Too many heart-pounding,
soul-searing,
crazy-ass mind movies
reek of nostalgia and fantasy
from that damn stench.
The smell of those sweet Marlboros,
The aroma I tasted with each kiss,
the scent I breathed in when I held you,
the flavor of you . . .
that awesomely beautiful,
smoky fragrance of you,
taunt me into dreadful yearning.
Damn Marlboros.

—Maureen Alexandra

Nihility

There is no stardust in my universe,
no bright lights glowing from light-years
away
there are only speckles of me, the dusty piss
verbiage
catapulted into the wild universal
nothingness, acrid nihility
decorated with emotional baggage
and insecurities.
There are no first, middle, or last words
obscuring views
just fanatical unconfined atoms spilling
from fervid wounds,
rocketed into the only place they might feel
welcomed,
a big fat void of incomprehensible nothing,
which truly is something

—Maureen Alexandra

Percussion

I feel the cascading tears,
liquid marbles tracing, following the labyrinth of
206 marrowed bones, paths of strengths. They say
jittery skeletons aren't real. They live only in the
dark crevices of the desperate underworld, aching
to be realized. But I see them. I feel them. I am
them. I hang, desperate, noosed, and grasping for
breath.
Rattle, rattle, roll. Grasp.
What is that sound but the dark destitution of
loneliness? An anxiety-filled display of unselfish
talent. Percussion at its finest. Jittery bones. Jitter
and quake. Drum roll please. Tum, tum, tum.
Beautiful music of a fearful soul. Devil's delight.
Let's dance, our horns upon our head, spirit half-dead. Lonely
xylophone crying, spirit of one
dying. Don't tell me it's all in my head. Just take
a look. You will see my dread.
Panic lives. Panic sings.
Rattle, rattle, roll. Grasp.

—Maureen Alexandra

HunnaHustla

Cheers to You

Unlike others I've known
Those whose voices like boredom drone
Your spirit conveys the ways you've honed
Laughing, loving, getting stoned
Living your life from skin to the bone
Thus of you shall I drink as I do my vodka
Deep, late at night, with pen and paper, alone
Writing of real-life moments shown . . .

—HunnaHustla

For You the Sun . . .

Shed your tears—for having loved
For tears are the light of your feeling
And even God's light cries on earth
As the poet's light cries on earth
Moonlight cries on earth
As starlight cries on earth
And tomorrow
Should tomorrow come
For you the sun shall cry its light . . .

—HunnaHustla

All That Is Beauty . . .

Like youthful laughter / a friend's surprise
Crashing waves / ocean tides
Pain of birth / a mother's cries
Sure as autumn falls
To winter's rise
All beauty
Fades
Dims
Dies

—HunnaHustla

It's Not You . . .

Not your fault
I'm not enough
One heart not enough
Not your fault, this stunted love, not enough
That its wings clipped, its path blocked
By neither you nor I
Not your fault being born to lie
Not your fault body rules your mind
Not your fault you cannot stay
Not your fault although I pray
Nor your fault
I cannot love
Your way . . .

—HunnaHustla

Tears for Mothers

Though uninspired, I write of you
As without you, this day, would not be mine too
For my breath is your breath, your gift to me
Every day I live
Is your life given free
Would only I live it better, my wish
Yet if you were here, your smile would say
"I love you still . . ."
Your eyes would pray
"In time you will . . ."
Your wish would be
Grieve not this day nor any day you see
As tears are for mothers . . .

—HunnaHustla

That Day without You . . .

The day blew cool upon the wind
I lay prone as shadows grew strong
And while unseen lives synchronized their song
My mood matched the day and the day seemed alone
As without you, your voice, without having you home
All were different, all seemed wrong, one a crowd, two a throng
Couldn't write, eating took too long, the dog missed you, I did too
Still I searched for inspiration, and before I was through
Day changed its mood from white-cloud gray to sundrenched hue
And . . . maybe, I too changed
As the day blew cool upon the wind
And earth-clouds covered the face of God . . .

—HunnaHustla

Still . . .

Why write, one may ask
Of awakening on morning to a light rainfall
It's . . .
Reminiscent of mine from her, that's all
Like having not slept, awaiting a word so small
Each raindrop her word, her call
Just . . .
Not the yes, I need to hear
Irony takes its place, I fear
Despite how often I've said
Dear . . .
All I am at your disposal, no matter all I am are words
Sometimes vain, sometimes wise, my best you will have
And know I've tried
That I'd rather wage war against ocean tide
Rather say I've cried and lost my pride
Rather banish my heart to cruel outside
Rather die than allow this vow denied
Still . . .
The irony being though only once I lied
The lie became our love's demise . . .

—HunnaHustla

Guest Poet: Joey Renee

"I wear my demons on my sleeve."

—Joey Renee

Lady Charming

Tall heels make me feel like a woman on top of the world
I'm a girl in love with fashion
I find it to be as artistic as a portrait of the words that I paint
With each stroke
Every word that I spoke
Was infused
Galactic Goddess
Is more than the shade of my lipstick
I'm made of much more than sugar and spice and everything nice
I'm eccentric, crazy, wild, smart, and curious
I can be blatant and dark
Dressed in all black with gold accents
Quite relentless with no repentance
A representation of the feelings
I wear on my sleeve
Extreme in everything I do
Sure I enjoy things in couture
You'll adore the beast inside this beauty
    A representation of what you want to see
Even if you somehow find it alarming
It's hard not to say I'm Lady Charming
Insanity knocks daily
Barely able to stop laughing
Breaking through a hollow mask
It's a task that my cool shades can handle
My torn and shredded jeans and distressed denim
In them
I'm oh so darling
Signed the not-so-cynical
Lady Charming

—Joey Renee

Love Comes with a Price

The lights shone brightly through the dark lit sky
I quiver as a chill is casted
The memory always outlasts the pain
It rains but only slightly
A little less than a drizzle
Without a cloud in the sky
The stars twinkled and glistened
I entered the venue
Threw my fur on the counter
Grabbed a ticket and a glass of wine
I was fine
Until I looked across the room and saw his face
It was a handsome face indeed
I was intrigued but not by his looks
They merely caught my attention
It was his intentions
It was his soul that I glimpsed
But only for a second
A second that grew shorter with each passing thought
Musicians pulling cords
Baristas serving much more than food for thought
Assuming this night would prove to be much more than sport
Resorting in another glass
Took another glance at this fellow
Becoming mellow as they began their first set
Analyzing was tantalizing,
Piercing and pulling them together
When he doesn't seem like much of anything at all
He was clean-cut and debonair
Without a care in the world
He didn't seem to have a girl or a wife
He seemed like a man on a mission to enjoy life
He had a thirst for it

Even worst that alone kept my attention
Knowing his full intention was to feed his ego
A lovely treat full of erotic stares and glares, compliments showered
Then deflowered
With absolutely zero solidarity
His eyes met no one's
Yet somehow he controlled the room
The same room in which he hardly took knowledge of
In that very room stood beautiful and exotic women of every background, shape,
And color
Yet he danced as if he knew not that all eyes were on him
They flocked
Still he mocked them with a glaring look of disapproval
You could see he was quite the amuser
It was a game
All the same this isn't a place for love
It's a place to chase your problems in the poison of your choice
While the musicians play a tune
Fitting for lost souls
I danced to a rhythm all my own
Fluent and effortless
Still I was intrigued by how he deceived the world around him
Wondering how a prize of his may perceive this night
Or how they should feel some level of fright on the night the prey fell
Or how they would assume a piece of his heart might suffice
Not knowing that although love comes to many
It always comes at a price
Another glass of wine with a long drag
Another gentleman asks if I need my coat
And I jokingly reply only if it comes with a smile
I look over to find him requesting a drink
One would think he's a man that enjoys his whiskey with no chase on the rocks
So I wasn't at all shocked when he asked for a Johnny Walker
He leaned over and whispered in my ear
"You don't seem like much of a talker"
I smiled and pulled my cigarette as I summoned the barrister

"I'm surprised I seem like anything to a mister such as yourself?"
Silence filled the air as he stared deeply into my eyes
Looking away
Although I found our interactions to be rather enlightening
But thoughts of a night with him are frightening
If I was able to feel him without a single touch
What could save me from his lust?
What could save me from the love he escaped?
Assuming one should negate any level of rationale
The thought was wild
While I was uninhibited
A cosmopolitan as he fetched my request
I took his hand implying yes
Allowing myself to fall in love for one night
I gave him my heart and it came at a price
Hauntingly beautiful like a night in Rome
Like a home you taking sanction of my heart
Cherished as a moment lost in time
It came with a price and that price was mine
Good-bye, lover

—Joey Renee

Warm Summers Glow

Sand between my toes
Staring through the eyes of a child
The smell of hot dogs in the air
It was up on Ridge Road
A favorite spot we would go
Swimming days with the family
Mom would take us to the deep end and spend hours of fun galore
With her we never knew what was in store
And no one could outswim Dad
I was glad, because it made him even more of a hero in my eyes
Man, I miss those summer nights
With never a care in the world
Just the breeze through your hair
And the sound of life all around you
Now you know
The warm summers glow
That is where you will find me on my darkest of days
Right there with my feet in the sand

—Joey Renee

HunnaHustla

For My Sorrow . . .

Dear old flames
Once along for the ride
Whose minds upon my swears relied
Whose passions later flickered and sighed
Forgive my youth for having said I love you
For even though words I had spoken with pride
They were often ruse uttered to bare your thighs
To indulge the many delights that had lain between
Or to at least be given sight of that sweet unseen
Still, which of you unbroken can attest I lied
As some poets believe lust a love when applied
Though perhaps to relieve guilt as I have tried
Thus, should I fear these words tomorrow?
That to kill a love is to kill a being
As hearts that have suffered
Have somewhat died . . .

—HunnaHustla

What Is It Like?

It is like a welcome home
To that first glass of cold chardonnay
Or like carefully selecting an ensemble
It's like the feeling you get when your smoothie
Has made you look younger
It's like writing prose and not giving a damn
Because it feels like poetry
That is what it's like
What being with you is like?
It's like you and I becoming us . . .

—HunnaHustla

Runaway Muse

"Muse everywhere, find another and use it . . ."
Your words, music, still your leaving I can't excuse it
For my heart, smitten, lives where poems are written
Wherein beating for you, when you had come
It had known there's no other as you are from
"And if another like me, then I am she . . ."
Your words, music, still your leaving I can't excuse it
For why pierce my soul
Your love
Only to leave me with memories of . . .

—HunnaHustla

Of Sunsets Calling

Ever felt a sunset calling
Envision its colors glorious sweep
Ever want its warmth to keep, shun need for sleep
To see that great ball peep behind mountains steep in oceans deep
Ever speed past sound to catch its light, to meet its grace just right
Ever depended upon tech to gauge its flight
Then be late seeing it fall
Toward night?

—HunnaHustla

Of Our Desolate Plight . . .

we
spawn of deity
rebelled against the gods
were banished to gloom and night
without a sun or moon in sight
where even day devoured light
now in tortured wretched souls we fight
not for good or evil, wrong or right
but to show our strength and might
how saddened we should be
of our desolate
plight . . .

—HunnaHustla

Writers Are . . .

Scribblers of unseen sights
Thrashing beneath walls of painted lights
Needing only, wanting only, sleep-filled nights
Awaiting its arrival is their unrelenting late fate
Pillows of goose down pounding windows of hate
Counting emotionless oceans at insomnia's gates
Their bag-lined eyes, ballooning in size
Blinded by their worded prize . . .

—HunnaHustla

Giselle . . .

Men made mad
By her face so fine
Artists painted her every line
Poets worded her as sublime
She played ballers into decline
Brought Wall-Streeters to welfare times
Many were jailed by her lips divine
Yet altogether their ruin
Less than mine . . .

—HunnaHustla

Guest Poet: Naschabella

"My spirit dances on this page with each breath of my words."

—Naschabella

Decrepit Dilapidation

Goodness leaned against
Evil's carcass and swooned.
She smiled at his
decrepit dilapidation.

—Naschabella

El Anafe

Idle hours next to the anafe with my grandma I sit,
engulfed in the air of the delicious aroma of guava
wood.
While the sweet beans simmered, my grandmother's
head in my lap did lay.
I inhaled the sweet cigar that she smoked and the rum
on her breath.
Told the tales of years gone by and what the future
would be like.

I laughed, a sound of youth and mirth, and slowly
caressed her brow.
Pincers in hand, one by one, I took out the gray hairs
framing her beautiful face.
Beautiful she was to me in those hours, the siesta!
Overflowing in the tranquility of our love, she smiled up
at me.
I knew, I was a product of that womb, being eaten away
by the MONSTER.
That is what she called cancer, the monster!
I could not envision her pain, I was not even ten, when
she weaved these tales.

She told me of beautiful, clean sidewalks where
pennies could be found.
Everywhere you looked in this city, I would be able to
see immense buildings that touched the sky . . .
New York . . . A new home . . . Far away from her and her
smell, the bouquet of love.
The joy of having this woman next to me, in my heart,
sings and lingers still.

As I look upon those peaceful days, my eyes look for
hers,
in a sky stabbed by brick buildings that make me
feel . . . Not even ten . . .
And as I pick up a penny in the dirty streets of this
Goliath,
my soul shouts out to the four winds.

They caressingly bring with them the fragrance of
yesteryears.
Her essence, that smell of guava root, sweet beans,
Tobacco, and rum touches me.
From far away it wafts and sweetly comes,
from the island where she rests, from her arms, from
her face, from her smile,
and her silken, raven-black mane delicately touched, by
angels, with gray . . .
Feeling the delicate touch
of my grandmother's spirit
caressing my brow, I smile.

—Naschabella

My Epeolatry

Poetry is deipotent.
Descrying visions in a glass of wine,
encountering dreams in the smoke
I exhale only to encapsulate them
in a sentence or verse that haunts
and keeps me awake.
My epeolatry is never morient for
perpetually my spirit yearns to sculpt
nature and humanity using words.
In my confabulation with a piece of
paper I find a lachrymogenic beauty
that shatters my soul.
This deceitful, benefic goddess is the
rataplan of my heart. In my idolatry
of poetry my mind attempts to disrobe
the pulchritudinous monstrosities of
life and impart them to the world.

—Naschabella

Never-Ending Search

When I have fears,
I take that worn path that
leads to yesteryear.
The sky blows downward.
My spiraling heart
that I had lost to eyes
I had never seen.
My soul relinquishes her hold
on that precious memory
of lips I never got to kiss.
I graciously walk my spirit
Toward the love I never felt.

—Naschabella

Ode to the Moon

Changeable moon,
illumined face caresses my fate
like sparkled grace.
Dance your magic in blackened skies,
while songs of mortals harmonize.

You're shifting time, moments, and sea
raining sweet promises to me.
Luna's gravitational pull
causes mass lunacy when full.

My demons in the garden wild,
loved you fiendishly deep and smiled.
Beings, swimming in disorder
round, pocked cinderblock moves water.

Your countenance dazzles the world
nightly with you my dreams unfurl.
While the wolves howl and the owls fly
Selene gifts poets the night sky.

—Naschabella

HunnaHustla

Jealous Toys

A child was I
When toys I loved
Thrown into a cathedral of cacti
Lay behind their vault of thorns
Like secret admirers
Laughing at my new love
Books . . .

—HunnaHustla

Never Say Never . . .

Never say never
But never will there ever be another as she
I could write all night about her being different in many ways
As never did I have to reach to hold her hand
Never say never but she had always taken mine
Never did I have to ask her to give me a call
She said, "Hello, it's me, I'm yours . . ."
Better than any song ever
Never had she failed to put her arms around me
She never let a harsh word or anger stand between us
Never thought she would leave or that life would take her from me
I could write all night about her as never
will there ever be another as she

—HunnaHustla

When It's Over . . .

Do you know a shift when you feel it a
friendship's end, a change of vibe?
When a love is over can you recognize that
"I'm leaving you" look in her eyes?
Do you destroy in rage, stomp about, do you cry,
Wondering why did she leave me, why did she go, why did she lie?
Although it is a cliché but when the chips
have fallen, all is said and done
Be willing to leave it at that
Forget saying good-bye
And shun . . .

—HunnaHustla

Forget Not . . .

You know a day will come
When they will show you as one
Drunk on attention they gave, words they rave
Where did you get it from, that I do weak, you strong
You forever right, I wrong, that I an outcast where you belong
To what magic did I succumb, commands I pen not mine your song
That I at your beck, your call, that your life lives large, mine small
Do you not recall, having gone up then fall, that I stood before all
Asserting you will climb that wall, should again limelight dim
Will you be with him, or he with another?

—HunnaHustla

Just Move On . . .

The door is open
And it is sometimes best to just move on
Don't even try to explain
Your pain, your restless, thought-filled nights
Nor the days, of endless, mindless, fights
Silence the lies that in the past you allowed to speak
The laughter, the rehearsed deceit
And though the eyes are endearing and deep
Turn from them
For despite love's joy, its bliss and happiness
There is an underlying surreality to it all
And it is sometimes best to just move on . . .

—HunnaHustla

Of Lessons Learned

From child to woman sublime, you learned in time
Of heat by touching fire, became trained by way of pain
You learned to have what you desire, you must work to gain
That an ocean rushing toward you wants only to come ashore
That small portions of a delicacy whets appetite for more
Learned to pity who lacks confidence in their endeavors
They cannot bring themselves to beat their own drum
You learned no woman a tramp, no man is a bum
Gift to one curse to some, old words become young
Yet now seems heaven denies skies their blue
For appears the gods have deemed this true
That if you are to learn loves ways too
You must with another one new
Let this one learn losing you

—HunnaHustla

93

Guest Poet: Shani Harris

"That moment when you know you have written a killer poem."

—Shani Harris

After Rain Falls

Water from streams flow
Flowers and dreams grow
Can you hear it?
The tiny droplets of pain dripping from everyone—from everywhere
Look how puddles of insecurities disappear

Sometimes the puddles are too filled up to be dried with mops
Because into each life, rain must fall
then we survive and strive—rainbows help us stand tall after the
pouring stops

Sun rays blaze through the cracks of dark clouds
brighter days are made, worries fade
We have survived the worst of our fears—God lives here in the bliss
the moment after rain falls

—Shani Harris

Beauty in Chaos

Can't find her muses
Paradise lost in still waters
She has drowned
Her mind still refuses but
The waves start moving
Will heaven be found?

Chaos in the pain
Chaos in her brain

Still there's beauty in chaos

Suffrage and bruises
Head trips lead to losses
Losses brought chaos
Chaos brought crosses
Praying day and night
She tosses
And turns
Slumber burns
Chaos is her name
Still there's beauty in chaos

—Shani Harris

Hurt Chains Broken

The chains are broken
Drums beat
Breaking the silence of the moment
Internal drums
The heart's language
Can you feel the rhythms?
Rising with each caress
With each kiss piercing with static stings
Impulse and temptations
Stimulation brings heat and heat brings fire
While fire spreads to desire and desires torment
Pupils dilate as if intoxicated palpitations
Is love spoken?

—Shani Harris

Loud and Clear

Let your tongue write me
Poems all over my body
Write me your favorite quotes
Play me like your favorite instrument
Make me hit all the notes
Let your skin paint my skin
Until I can't tell mine from yours then stop
Make me beg then give me more
While your fingertips explore
Sincerely and silently
We don't need to speak
We'll do it quietly
But
These are just stories my eyes tell yours from across the room
See volumes are spoken in every glance we share
In this feverish lust
I hear love loud and clear

—Shani Harris

HunnaHustla

Of What I Wish I Had Said

I wish I had said you are right and I wrong
That without you days will be short / my nights long
That counting hours of your leaving / hoping time deceiving,
My unseen grieving will deny you're gone
Wish I had said what I wanted to hear / that losing you is what I fear
That without us, we, you and me, what is joy, bliss, togetherness
If not love, what is above, happiness / I wish I had asked and then
said
This love you gave / my life it saved / without it, I'm a coward not
brave
Enough to allow my heart be read in the manner of words I've bled
Yet even though I walk in the ways you've led
Even though you softened the path I've tread
Even though still I feel your zeal
And I your absence dread
Much have I left
Unsaid . . .

—HunnaHustla

Of What I've Lost . . .

With scarf in her hand / she stood in door way
Debating what I cannot say / but that portal yet stares
A malevolent angry way / whether accusing or asking
"What pain filled memory dared pierce her hear?"
I again cannot say
She turned, and like an omen its come to be
An errant hair broke free,
Clung to her neck as if she were leaving
Sun in her eyes shed no light on her thoughts
I looked away, looked back, only her scarf remained
Now every step past that door reminds of what I've lost
: Of what I've lost and hope to gain ...

—HunnaHustla

To Hush Regrets

My song for her, I never sang it
My poem for her, I never wrote it
My love for her, I never gave it
Still on the last day I clung to her
As dark tonight
Letting go only to leave
Speaking solely to say good-bye
And to hush regrets . . .

—HunnaHustla

In Reflection . . .

Do ever you think of them,
Now they've gone,
The loves you've known?

Would they of you, if you were they?

Now both you've gone,
Is each your lives at peace?

Or as torn as one
As once
As two

—HunnaHustla

Guest Poet: James H. Brown III

"That's why I was built with emotions; so I can feel Him [God] . . ."

A Soldiers Poem

All is quiet
All is still
And stays that way
Till we reach the hills

But then
A riot
Gunfire ablaze and a burst of rounds
Cause my eyes to gaze

In our trenches
Down below
Soldiers fall
From the Russians blow

Yet
On we press and I take a breath
As I run into certain death
It's these times I think of my mother
While I shoot to kill another brother

Drafted in
No choice to choose
While on this battlefield
We all lose
Fighting the government's fight
As I wonder if it's my last night

Then with the second wave
I feel the blow
My rifle falls
As I let go
My body's heavy and chest is numb
And so I fear that my time has come

As I lay here looking at sky
And the bullets keep on whizzing by
I wonder if I'm going home
Or if I'm doomed to die alone

Brothers, husbands, cousins and kin
All I've killed
I'll repay my sins

For every tear the widows have wept
My scarlet blood is a drop less kept
And as my eyelids now feel heavy
I have no choice
But my soul is ready

--James H. Brown III
United States Navy
Sunrise: 12/08/1990
Sunset: 08/29/2015
Written At Age 14

Collaborations

Stimulus

In the mornings
Your eyes are green for me
You hold me
Like the last spring bud on the cusp

—Fabienne Casseus

Response

Holding bloom
Till evening dusk
You wait for me

Like falling stars with bated breath
Savor moonbeams before their death
You kiss me

Your voice silent as mountains oceans deep
Whispers even in your sleep
You miss me

Cherishing all you give
Whether it withers or lives
I'll love thee . . .

—HunnaHustla

Stimulus . . .

The half question makes me stir,
Stomach churns,
While I sit, tip, on the precipice,
Of my seat.
Heart pounds as thoughts abound,
Afraid you've made me out,
Tipping toward the catechism,
Of what ifs.

—Kaela Renee

Response . . .

. . . and what if
We should topple off this precipice, this love
What if our descent should end as it has before
With your voice pleading innocent
My mind shouting your name
What if
My soul yearns for yours in such a death
What if yours should long for mine
Knowing love is what took our breath
What if our hearts decline to pine
Desires to build a new love shrine
What if we choose to live
This time?

—HunnaHustla

Guest Poet: Kaela Renee

"Passion is the fire that will ignite, making everyone's lives shine brighter."

—Kaela Renee

Botticelli Baby

I'll be your Botticelli baby,
If you don't mind the curves,
The folds and the pale skin, the wild wavy hair,
Falling around this long arching neck.
I'll be your Beethoven's symphony,
If you'll be Ludwig, deaf,
Unable to hear this voice that hums discordantly,
Yes, unable to sing a chord I repeat inadequate,
But in the moonlight dear,
I'll have you singing hallelujah,
At the melodic way I praise your fingers, play on.
I'll be your Shakespearean sonnet,
Pray, pay close attention to the rhythm of my heart,
A rose is not a rose, a kiss is not a kiss,
In my heart the message of the matter lies,
The vulnerability in the meter of my expression,
And will you appreciate the flow,
The artistry of sharing what mysteries I have hidden in my heart,
These tantalizing metaphors and romantic visions,
I share with you?

—Kaela Renee

Chest Pain

Her breath is timed deeply,
I can hear it,
Filling the silence of this dark hall,
Door opened,
My heart aches at the sorrow,
The pain in every exhale,
As if she's trying to get a grip,
But fingers slip,
And she's nothing more than human,
Falling into sleep,
The only release to the scrutiny she bares,
Keeping her head above water,
Desperately living,
Breath deep but short, gasping at peace in attempts,
At calming the raging war within her mind,
Pressing her insides to turn against personal willpower,
Tissue inflamed with every pent-up sigh,
Heart beating against too tight bars,
Bruised and barely able to escape,
Drums thumping robotically,
Despite her itching hands to quicken the beat.

—Kaela Renee

Lips

I like the feeling of lips,
Brushing, nuzzling into the curve of
my neck,
Gently caressing my jaw with
affections,
Touching my cheeks, tempting,
The feeling of them pressed against
mine,
This euphoria I can't hide.
I like lips, the tingles down my spine.
Hair on my neck rise,
I admit it, I like to be kissed.

—Kaela Renee

Mother Nature

Nature knows no subtlety,
Knows no restraint,
Nor master.
At the mercy of her enigmatic emotions,
Gratitude fills my heart,
The early rays of golden light touch my face,
A gentle hand stroking my cheek.
I surrender to the graceful breeze,
Tousling my ebony hair,
As if to say "Be free, my love."
Should I?
I daresay my mind has no clue,
I have been swept away already,
Carried off by the wind,
To ride on sunbeams,
Far across land and sea,
And shall again I ever find it again?

—Kaela Renee

Tiptoe Habits

Tiptoe habits die hard
Raising as if gravity releases me
From its charge,
Giddiness forces my toes to tip,
My heels reaching for the sky

—Kaela Renee

HunnaHustla

The Gift

Woman
You heal my mind with words of yours
You awaken my spirit with yours
My soul with yours
You silence eyes with those of yours
You adorn my life with yours . . .

—HunnaHustla

Strange Be This Love

I confess that I love you
A strange love, this love, merely resting within me
Demanding only to be expressed, this once, in this manner
Yes, it even dictates the manner of its own expression
Asking naught of my heart, but snatching my pen

Strange, be this love, strange

For though it lives unrequited I grow not weak
And although knowing it exists provides a moment of joy
This … joy … does not pleasure me

Strange love

In that I clung to past loves, I admittedly held tight
Was unreasonably unwilling to let go
But here strange in this love I am willing
Should your release be your desire and …
If such be

I will not wail through tears your name in the night
While blue songs sing
And soft rains fall
Staccato-like
Against the walls
Of both my heart and home
I will not cling to memories of your well-turned phrases
Your colored pictures in black and white
I won't dream of your gold flecked eyes
Or long to mine them for clues to your soul
I will not listen in dark at times
For the tingle of your chimes
Nor for the laughter in your voice

No deja vue
For the look once given by you, to me
That I took to be
Perhaps foolishly
The look of love
I will not dwell upon glances stolen by me of your smile
Nor will I cast
In the bronze of my thoughts
Even a simile of your being
Though yet
In this reflection through lilt and rhyme
I confess that I love you

A strange love, this love …

As in past romance I did possess and was possessed
My love choked and was choked
And the feeling grew weak
Feeding the need for lies
With every deceit

Love became pale in the face of toxic jealousy
While I
Stood by
Like a helpless doctor
Watching over a dying patient
Having not the antitoxin for saving the life of my love
I cried out
Yes!
I cried
To the supreme doctor
"God, remove this hurt from my heart …!"

Then in answering cure of my amorous affliction
I became aware of my heart's addiction
To its own
Weakness
For love

Thus

Strange be
This love
Strange …

––HunnaHustla––

Edwards Brothers Malloy
Oxnard, CA USA
March 1, 2016